Poems from the Heart

BETH J. ROGERS

WESTBOW
PRESS®
A DIVISION OF THOMAS NELSON
& ZONDERVAN

This book is a work of non-fiction. Unless otherwise noted, the author and the publisher make no explicit guarantees as to the accuracy of the information contained in this book and in some cases, names of people and places have been altered to protect their privacy.

WestBow Press books may be ordered through booksellers or by contacting:

WestBow Press
A Division of Thomas Nelson & Zondervan
1663 Liberty Drive
Bloomington, IN 47403
www.westbowpress.com
1 (866) 928-1240

Because of the dynamic nature of the Internet, any web addresses or links contained in this book may have changed since publication and may no longer be valid. The views expressed in this work are solely those of the author and do not necessarily reflect the views of the publisher, and the publisher hereby disclaims any responsibility for them.

Any people depicted in stock imagery provided by Getty Images are models, and such images are being used for illustrative purposes only. Certain stock imagery © Getty Images.

ISBN: 978-1-9736-2754-8 (sc)
ISBN: 978-1-9736-2755-5 (e)

Library of Congress Control Number: 2018905356

Print information available on the last page.

WestBow Press rev. date: 06/19/2018

To my Father God, my Lord and Savior, Jesus Christ, and the Holy Spirit. May every word written bring glory and honor to You.

To my grandmothers, Bernice Hyams and Myrtle Jackson, who loved the Lord Jesus Christ and passed down Christian values to my parents and me.

To my father, Bill Jackson, and my mother, Paula Dukes, who raised me in a Christian home. You both have always loved and encouraged me in all that I have done. I cherish your wisdom and advice. I love you both so much.

To my husband, Mike Rogers, for we are one in Christ. Thank you for always being by my side and loving me. I will always love you.

To our adult children, their spouses, and our granddaughter: Micah, Todd, and Makenna; Colton and Jodi. All of you love the Lord and serve Him. I am truly blessed. I love you all.

To my brother, Billy Jackson; his wife,Robin and my nieces, Brittany and Brooke.Thank you for all your love and support.

To my sister-in-law, Jacquelynn Vickers, who kept encouraging me to write this book of poems. You never let up. Thank you for believing in me.

To Caitlyn Rowell. God sent you at just the right time. Thank you for all of your help.

Contents

Preface

The Holy Spirit moves on us at different times and in different seasons of our lives. God is always talking to us, if we will just listen. God just wants to spend time with us. He wants to share His heart with us and love on us. He is our heavenly Father, and He desires our fellowship. He looks forward to the moments in time when we just sit at His feet and enter into His presence. God often speaks to me poetically, and I write. He speaks to me prophetically, and I write. Sometimes I question the words I put on paper, but as I read them, I know that they are not my words but God-inspired words. The Bible is the only true written Word of God, and it is not to be added to or taken away from. The Holy Spirit is my helper, my comforter, my counselor, and my guide. He encourages me, though my writing, to uplift those who are hurting, edify the body of Christ, and lead those who are lost to Jesus. As you read, may each poem reflect my Father's love and my Father's heart.

Introduction

Today is the day.

Each day that we wake up is another blessed day that the Lord has made, just for us!

We are the apple of His eye.

We are His love.

He delights in our presence.

He awaits our fellowship, and He loves us with a love that is not carnal. A love where He would die for us, a cruel and agonizing death, so that we could walk in victory and have eternal life.

This collection of poems is a reflection of the goodness of God. His heart speaks and tells of His love, His goodness, His mercy, His grace, and His faithfulness. May you sense His presence as you read each poem, and may the Holy Spirit bring comfort, peace, and joy to your heart and soul.

Reflection

As a diamond sparkles when light shines on its face,
That is how Jesus reflects in you
When you give Him first place.
Let Him shine in your life.
He will bring you much joy
And shower you with blessings you cannot contain.

Today

Order my steps today, Lord.
Let my path always lead to You.
Direct my life toward righteousness,
Always bearing fruit anew.
Give me what I need today.
May we walk side by side.
I will live each day with a grateful heart;
Trusting and obeying in you, I will abide.
You have already given me
All I need for each day.
May I be humble and kind to others,
Seeing others with your eyes of love, I pray.
Let me live today with a compassionate heart,
One that spreads love to all those around,
Hoping that others will see Jesus in me
And praying in Christ may they be found.
Another day will come and go,
And as I reflect on the things I have done,
I pray, Lord, that I have pleased you
From morning's sunrise till the setting of the sun.

A Clean Heart

Clean my heart today, Lord.
Make it new.
Soften up the hardness there.
Melt it to be more like You.

Let love, mercy, and grace
Overtake this once-hard heart of mine.
Mold it into a new heart
Overflowing with Your love divine.

Cast away all the fear
And replace it with faith,
For then I can live in peace,
And rest in Your amazing grace.

Hold my heart so close to Yours
That our beats are in sync,
And as I go about my day,
Together may our hearts link.

Then fear will be no more.
Only love exuberates from me,
My heart new and complete.
So as I go about each day,
May Your heart beating in me
Others see.

My Day

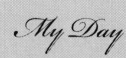

I praise You, Lord, with my whole heart.
My love for You will never part.
Each day I wake, I will honor You
With a prayer of thanksgiving and worship too.

Let me sit at Your feet.
Let me talk with You.
Let me silently listen to Your voice,
Speaking wisdom anew.

As I wait and listen within,
I rest in Your faithfulness again.
Once again, this is the beginning of my day,
When I seek You and pray.

So as I go about my way,
May I live my life today
To glorify and honor You. Lord,
In all I do and say.

I Am Free

Sometimes I get down,
And sometimes I get blue,
Knowing that I should not
Because, Lord, I believe in You.

For there is no reason
For me to be oppressed.
May heart echoes that You love me.
So why am I upset?

The things of this world that I see and hear
Pull my spirit down.
Even though I know You are near,
My flesh holds me bound.

This carnal walk of life.
That I go about each day
Sometimes is a struggle
Because fear gets in the way.

But, Lord, when I reflect
On all You have done for me,
I no longer can stay depressed,
For You won my victory.

You paid the price for my happiness.
Joy and peace You bought for me.
So now my spirit arises in my soul
As my heart cries, "I am free!"

Ways

Forgive me, Lord,
For my ways
That may displease You
And corrupt my days.
There is no excuse.
No reason to find.
But only selfishness and being unkind.
My heart gets hard.
My spirit gets slack
As my walk with You comes under attack.
Evil spirits are lurking at my back.
But You, Lord, are before me,
Always convicting and teaching me Your way.
If I will just repent,
You will clear up my day
And bring back to my heart and mind
Peace restored
As I cry out to You, my Savior and Lord.

My Faith

Lord,
Let my faith in You carry me.
May I have the strength of a palm tree,
Bending in the storms and the wind,
Remaining stronger than I have ever been.

Not worn, nor battered through the gale,
But firm and strong I will prevail.
Though the winds blow around me, I will stand.
Your mercy protects me from sinking sand.

And when the storm passes, I will say,
"Lord, You have kept me strong today."

I will still be standing like the palm tree
When others are knocked down.
Your grace and mercy hold me up
On solid ground.

Through trial and test,
My faith in God does not fold.
My anchored roots forever hold.

Your Instrument

On this instrument that You have created,
I will express my love for You.
This melody that I sing,
May it help to carry me through.
Let it be pleasing unto Thee,
Always echoing the same.
The words flowing from my mouth,
Bringing glory to Your name.

As I sing, as I sing,
Let my true heart anthems ring.

I have a place for You
Among this flesh of mine.
That place is hidden in my heart,
Not in my carnal mind.
From down deep in my soul,
Your praises rise above.
My heart is the only place
That filters Your true love.

As I sing, as I sing.
Let my true heart anthems ring.

If I have not told You lately,
Nor stopped to honor You,
May I take this moment now, Lord,
To express my gratitude.
As I lift my voice to You, Lord,
I will bless Your holy name.
Not with my mind, nor my flesh.
But my spirit will proclaim.

With my lips, I lift my voice and give You heartfelt praise.
My love for You grows more and more as I live out my days.

Quiet Time

In my quiet time,
I can sense Your presence.
In my quiet time,
I Know You are near.
In my quiet time,
I can talk to You.
In my quiet time,
I have faith You hear.

A Moment of Time

In the stillness of Your presence, Lord,
I listen for Your voice.
I wait patiently to hear You
Whisper secrets to me.

I love to be in Your presence,
For there, peace and rest can be found.
I love to wait and sense
Your love all around.

So why do I want to walk away?
Why do I think of all the things I must do in my day?
When all of my peace and all of my rest
Can be captured …

In a moment of time.
In a moment of time, You brighten my day.
In a moment of time, You wash all my fears away.
In a moment of time, I can praise Your name.
In a moment of time, Your goodness I can proclaim.
In a moment of time, I can seek Your face.
In a moment of time, I can sense Your grace.
In a moment of time, I can call out to You.
In a moment of time, I know what I must do.
In a moment of time, You cleanse my heart.
In a moment of time, I know Your love for me will never depart.
In a moment of time, hope comes alive.
In a moment of time, I know I will survive.

He Is Listening

Have I not told you?
It is not true.
Your life is in Christ Jesus.
He will carry you through.

From generation to generation,
Times past, old, and new.
Jesus is the same yesterday, today, and forever.
He will always be there for you.

Kneel before the Lord and with unveiled eyes see.
He is your heavenly Father.
And He will listen intently.

He can hear you loud and clear.
He has the answers to your questions,
If you just draw near.

Do not fret or worry.
Cast all your cares with bended knee,
And the peace Christ paid for at Calvary's cross
Will set your heart and mind free.

Abide

Lord, You fill my darkest hour.
Lord, You satisfy my soul.
Lord, You shine Your light upon me.
Lord, You make me whole.

When the waves of life keep crashing
And the winds blow bittersweet,
You wash away my tears
When I sit at Your feet.

In the stillness,
In the quiet of my day,
I wait for You to speak
As I listen to what You say.

I know that with each moment
I spend alone with You,
I find hope and peace in Your presence.
My faith arises, and I am renewed.

I wait patiently.
Though with my eyes I cannot see,
I hear You, Lord,
Softly speaking to me
As I listen with my heart
And turn off the sounds that surround me.
You gently speak
Like the calmness of the sea.
For when my soul is quiet
And all distractions are set aside,
That is when I commune with You,
And together we abide.

Shadows

When shadows fall around you
And you know not what to do,
Look to your Father God,
For He cares for you.
No situation is ever too vast
For Him to undertake.
He created the heavens and the earth,
And they were no mistake.
Darkness and shadows prevail all around,
But under His loving wings, safety can be found.
Signs of the times only show this to be true;
Your life must be in Christ to carry you through.
He will overshadow you
If you only let Him in,
Into your prayer closet.
He wants to come in,
For there He can garnish your mind
With peace to remain sane.
There He can protect you
From all your hurt and pain.

Behind the Scenes

The Lord works behind the scenes
Where no one sees or hears.
His mercy is ever flowing down from heaven,
Even though we may be shedding tears.
He said He will not leave us.
He is with us through it all.
His loving wings of mercy are there
To catch us when we fall.
He knows that we have eyes to see,
And we hear the enemies' lies unfold.
But if we just get a grip,
The blinders will crumble and fall.
Yes, God works behind the scenes.
No matter what we see or hear,
Our faith and trust in Him
Must override all doubt and fear.
The Word must be spoken into the atmosphere.
A two-edged sword, the Word of the Lord our ears must hear.
The Bible is God's Word, spoken to all,
To fight in the spirit realm, to break down every wall.
Fear has no place to stand up against God's Word.
But with our ears we must hear and let His Word be heard.
Speak to the mountains loud and clear.
Let all hear the victory and promise without fear.
For when faith arises in our soul,
To connect with our heart and mind,
Then God's grace and love settle in,
And there His peace we find.

He Is Strong

When trials and tribulations come,
    and everything seems to be going wrong,
        it may just be the perfect opportunity
           for God
              to show Himself strong.

Trust

I will trust in You, Lord.
I will lay all my cares at Your feet.
For I know deep down in my spirit
My soul You will keep.

I will trust in You, Lord,
No matter what may come my way.
You said You have a plan and a purpose for me
Each and every day.

I will trust in You, Lord,
To stay on the path You designed for me.
To walk out my life on this earth.
To be what You called me to be.

I will trust You, Lord.
And to my own understanding I will not lean.
As I am led by Your Holy Spirit.
May my faith in You be seen.

Cares

I cast my cares on You, Lord.
I lay all of my burdens at Your feet,
For I know, Lord,
My needs You will meet.

This life on earth is temporary,
And I fret and war with stress all day long.
But if I fix my eyes on You, Jesus,
I soon realize all my cares are gone.

Jesus, you have already taken my cares.
But I must lay my burdens at Your feet.
For then and only then will I realize
The victory was already won, complete.

Cares of this life will repeat.
But I will kneel before You, Jesus, without defeat.
I will cast the cares and burdens that come my way
And let You, Jesus, give me peace today.

Surely

If God can part the Red Sea,
He can surely take care of me.
No mountain is too high,
No valley too low
For Him to extend His hand of mercy.
The Bible tells me so.
He holds me in the palm of His hand
And shields me from the storms of life.
He carries me in His loving arms
Though the day and through the night.
When I feel that hope is lost
And fears surround my every thought,
He shows up at just the right time,
And in Him my help I find.
My trust in Him never leaves my spirit,
Although my mind does not always believe so.
The longer I live for Him,
My faith in God does grow,
In the natural and in the spirit.
The storms in life bring about change.
My hope in God is sure,
Just like the sun coming out after the rain.

Mercy

After the storm is gone,
The clouds slowly fade away.
The winds die down.
Calmness awakes.
The leaves fall to the ground.

The air is fresh and alive,
Although I see destruction caused by the wind.
The sun breaks through the clouds,
Assuring me it will come out again.

There is a peace now
That comforts my soul,
One that had not been there
Though the storm's destruction and toil.

Hope and faith settle back down into my heart,
For my God once again
Has brought me through the dark.

With each passing storm,
My spirit arrests my thoughts
To what is important in my life on earth.

Not things, titles, or possessions.
Only Mercy that comes from my Savior.
Nothing else can measure its worth.

Cornerstones

The cornerstone who was rejected
Today does not stand alone,
For there are many small cornerstones
Who go about and roam.
They take God's Word
And go from place to place,
Sharing His perfect love
To every tribe and race.
For these little stones
Whom we think are so incomplete
Are sharing the gift of love
To the humble and the meek.
Even though they may seem unnoticed
In this world's sight,
They are telling of a great treasure
And are shining a brilliant light,
The light of the Gospel,
The Good News,
God's Word.
For unto many people and nations,
Their words are heard.
So continue on your journey,
Little cornerstones,
Knowing that in Christ
You never stand alone.

One Second

It only takes one second in all of your life on earth,
to say, "Forgive me, Lord," and Jesus will come into your heart
and change everything in your life for good.

Harvest

Hurry

All.

Run

Valiantly.

Every

Sinner

Turn.

Jesus Is Lord

Jesus is Lord.
He is the only one.
He gave His life for us.
He is God's only Son.

He did not have to die for us.
No, He could have walked away.
But He saw our future.
He saw our road.
He saw our imperfect way.

He gave His life through obedience.
He gave all that He could give.
He became our Lord and Savior.
And with Him we shall forever live.

Praying

All over the world,
People kneel and pray,
Praying for a move of God
In this last and final day.
They cry with their hearts
And petition Jesus to come.
But it is not quiet time.
For His work is not yet done.
For there is still much to do.
There is still much to be.
So continue praying on your knees
And talk to God in prayer.
Know that He is always listening,
And His return is drawing near.

Love

Love covers a multitude of sins
And convicts hearts within.
No other force is so strong and true.
No other force will satisfy you.
God's love sent His Son to the cross,
And He paid the ultimate price for the loss.
Jesus did it all at Calvary,
To set your heart and mind free.
Take hold of His love today
And turn from your wicked way.
Greater love has no other than He.
He gave His life freely.

Mighty Rush

There's a mighty rush of God's Spirit now, and it's calling you alone.
There's a mighty rush. Can you feel it now? It's flowing from God's throne.

There's a quiet hush. Can you hear it now? It's calling you today.
There's a quiet hush. Listen closely now and hear what the Spirit says.

It's calling you today,
For God has made a way.
He paid the price for you to be free.
Just turn to Him and say,
"Lord, I want to walk Your way,"
And He will be waiting for you.

The Way

For some reason,
I do not always know what to say.
Because of intimidation,
I do not share with others
The way.

The way to eternal life in Jesus Christ.
He is the only Savior and giver of life.
No other one can save a sinner's soul from hell.
So why do I hesitate to tell?

Jesus gave His life for all humankind,
To free one's spirit and one's mind.
Ask Him to be Lord of your heart today,
And He will lead and guide your life.
And Jesus will show you
The way.

Open Your Heart

Awake, for your redemption draws nigh.

Open your heart.
Let Jesus in to give you a new start.
Cry out to him.
Now is the time.
He did it all for you,
So you did not have to.

Time to awake.
Do not hesitate.
Open up your heart now
And let Jesus Christ in.
Let His sacrifice bring healing from within.

Open your heart!

Paid

No, you were not there
When they nailed Him to the tree.
You were not there
To see his suffering.
No, you were not there
When they pierced His side.
You were not there
When He cried.
No, you were not there
When they took him down from the cross.
You were not there,
When it appeared He suffered loss.
No, you were not there
When He arose from the grave.
Do you really know
The price He paid?

Trip of a Lifetime

When Jesus splits the eastern sky,
There won't be found a dry eye.
Those rising upward, joyfully crying.
Those left behind, stunned and sighing.
Day of all days!
Event of all events!
Moment of all moments!
Time of all times!
Has come.
Will you be ready for that day?
The trip of a lifetime, you could say.
Did you accept Jesus as your Savior and Lord?
For He already paid your ticket, one you couldn't afford.
I hope and pray
That you made it right
And shared His story
Day and night!

Zacchaeus

There once was a man who climbed up a sycamore tree.
He wanted to see the man from Galilee.
But he did not know; he could not foresee.
The plan God had for him would be his destiny.
So he climbed up high, out of the way, where Jesus could not see.
Zacchaeus, just a simple man, like you and me.
But as the Savior passed his way, Zacchaeus did not know
Jesus was watching him, and He was not going to let him go.
"Zacchaeus," He said, "come down from that tree.
Come on down today and talk with Me.
I have come to give you eternal life. I have come to save your soul.
Just come on down and turn your life around, and I will make you whole.
Zacchaeus, why are you hiding from Me? Come on down from that sycamore tree.
I want to talk with you. I have come to save your soul. Let's walk and talk together, my friend,
And I will make you whole."
There are many in this world today who are hiding up in a tree,
Looking down at the Savior, wanting to be free.
He is calling you today.
He is waiting to save your soul.
Come on down. Let Jesus turn your life around, and He will make you whole.

Heaven

Jesus is the cornerstone.
He alone can take us home
To the place where all heavenly hosts await,
Our entrance through His holy gate.

God does not take us.
He calls us home.
He does not make us sick.
He never leaves us alone.

This life on earth is hard.
And each day we live may be tough.
Live to honor God,
For He is always enough.

Our hope is in Christ.
Doubt brings us down.
God's love lifts.
And there, trust and peace are found.

Look to Christ Jesus today,
For in the twinkling of an eye,
Our hope of heaven awaits us,
In that very moment
When we tell this earth goodbye.

Are You Ready?

Are you ready?
Are you ready to see the Lord?
Are you ready?
Are you ready to greet the Lord?
For the time is drawing near,
And He is shortly to appear.
Are you ready to meet the Lord?

For the Lord is coming soon, sooner than you may know.
The days are going by quickly; the nights are no longer long.
The clock is ticking faster, for it is soon the hour to go home.

For the sky will burst open wide, and every eye will see
Jesus coming down from heaven, coming for you and me.
But if your heart is hard and you have never let Him in,
That day will be filled with terror, for you know that it is the end.

You ponder deep within, *Without Jesus, I'm not complete.*
Suddenly a wave of glory hits you and knocks you to your feet.
Everything you have been told about God quickly flashes before your eyes.
The blinders lift. No more lies.

And as you lie there in disbelief and fright, the sky
will turn dark, and there will be no light.
For the lights have been taken out, and you have been left behind.
Feelings of despair and emptiness fill your heart and mind.

At that moment, you realize that Jesus was the only way.
So listen to what I have to say:
Make it right with God today!

Love Is God

Love never fades.
It never comes to an end,
Never grows weary,
And frees all from sin.
Love reaches to the mountaintops
And to the valleys low.
Love mends our hearts with friends again
Who had become a foe.

Love changes everything.
Love changes the atmosphere.
Faith arises in our soul.
Instead of doubt and fear,
Love lifts us out of the miry clay
Where hopelessness abounds.
God's love for us sent Jesus to earth.
In Him our hope is found.

Love lifts. Love encourages.
Love lights up our heart within.
Without it, the world grows darker into sin.
Love has no limits. No boundaries. No walls.
Love reaches far and wide,
To the great and small.

Love is God, and God is love.
Love was sent down from Him above.
God gave us Jesus.
No greater love than this you'll find
To wash away the sins of all humankind.

My Heart

Poems are usually written about life and love.
This collection came to me from heaven above.

God's Creation

The sky is blue.
The sun is a yellow burst of fire.
The sea aqua and clear.
The mountaintops display splendor and height.
The moon glows its dimming light.

Getting Up

Oh, Lord, how I toss and turn
before the sun comes up.
If you want me to get out of bed, good luck!
My bed is so cozy, so warm and so soft.
I do not want to get up—no, not at any cost.
It is still dark and cold outside.
The sun has not yet decided to shine.
So why do you want me to get out of my bed?
Please let me just lay here and whine.
Who made the day begin so early?
For once, the old rooster did crow.
For then I knew the time to rise.
No clock had to tell me so.
But time has not changed.
The earlier I rise, the more work I can get done.
So once again, I will set my alarm
And wake up without the sun.

At the Beach

I love to walk and talk with You, Lord,
At my favorite place:

The beach.

Ocean waves crashing.
The sound so calming and tranquil.
The smell of the sea delightful
As the wind blows abruptly.
Seashells and moist sand
Squeeze between my toes.
These are just a few reasons why
My love for the beach grows.

Lend a Hand

Be kind.
Oh, can you do that?
Is it so hard to lend a hand
To a fellow man?

For if you do,
You will feel so good inside,
And God's love and grace
Will within you reside.

God Sees Everything

Somewhere in life's shadows,
Evil lurks, without a sound.
In the darkness, people do bad things
And think no one is around.
But as the light shines from above,
The shadows disappear.
Always know God sees everything.
His light makes all things clear.

Lessons

Godly lessons are often learned

When we least expect them to be.

For when things don't go the way we want,

A lesson may follow immediately.

We learn from our mistakes.

And we learn even though we may fail.

But with each lesson learned,

We mature to much avail.

Mother's Day

Mother's Day would be no day
If I had not you
To reflect on all the memories past
That have been made between us two.
The joy and the laughter
Of all the years we share.
Spending time with each other,
Cherishing all of your love and care.

Of all the mothers that I have known,
You rise above them all, you alone.

You have always given of yourself
So unselfishly in every way,
From putting my wants and needs above yours,
And that always being okay.
So with heartfelt love and appreciation,
With pen in hand,
I just want to say
I love you, Mom, and always will
Each and every Mother's Day.

Thanksgiving

As I stirred in the kitchen,
The day before the big feast,
I thought and I reminisced of Thanksgivings past,
To say the least.

Why was I so excited
At this special time of year?
Maybe, I thought,
Because loved ones would be near.

I pondered on why I wanted to make some calls
To my family and friends.
Was it because of the anticipation of the holidays?
Or maybe a time to make amends.

My heart seemed warm and kind
As I reflected on Thanksgivings past
Playing in my mind.

So much to do, so much to prepare.
Could I get it all done without despair?

Then it came to me
Out of somewhere.
Why did I cook and bake?
Why did I care?

Thinking how frantically I felt
To make a Thanksgiving dinner complete and all done,
I realized it wasn't just about eating
But about the fellowship and fun.

It's not about the cooking and the baking
That we celebrate
But the time we spend together preparing,
No matter if we eat early or late.

It's not about the big meal
That makes our heart's complete
But the time we spend together,
When we all meet,
And being thankful to the Lord above
For sending us Jesus and His love.

It's the gathering together of family and friends
Who are still alive and living.
That is why we come together and celebrate
Another Thanksgiving.

Christmas Day

On this Christmas Day,
At this time of year,
My heart listens quietly to, You, Lord.
What must I hear?
The sounds and noises
Are constantly stealing me away
To a time of year
That is Your special day.
The hustle and bustle.
The people so many,
Spending money, even their last penny,
On stuff and on things,
Trying to fill a void in their hearts
That only You, Lord Jesus, can fill.

I sometimes feel so empty,
Looking for satisfaction and fulfillment in everything around.
But only in You, Jesus, can peace be found.
For only in You, Lord, is my true purpose known.
Only in my faith and hope in You alone.
So as I turn off all the noise around,
I look to You, my Father,
for in You I am found.
You are the only one, Jesus, who can take my sins away.
You are the only one who can brighten my day.
You are the reason that I live.

To You my life I do give.
My hope and my purpose are in You alone.
My expectation of my heavenly home,
Where one day soon
I can leave this messed-up world behind
And finally throughout eternity
Have peace of mind.
And when that day comes,
Jesus, my journey here will be complete.
And finally face-to-face, Lord,
We will meet.

The Gift

In the town of Bethlehem one cold winter's night,
A baby child was born.
The stars were shining bright.
The people did not know what had taken place.
But a Savior had been born into the world, to save the human race.
Questions arose about the child, and rumors spread abroad.
Was this really the Savior, the Lord and King of all?
Yes, it was true, this event had truly taken place.
God had given His greatest gift to everyone who would receive.
For all that was required of them was that they just believe.
People still question this unusual and awesome event.
They still wonder and reason what was really meant.
What was the purpose and what was the plan?
The answer is very simple.
His name was Jesus Christ, and it is still Jesus today.
Though many have tried to discredit Him, but they were taken away.
He is the Savior of the world, the Lord and King of all.
He came, was born, died, and raised to save the great and small.
But many still turn away and receive not the gift
that was given that Christmas night.
They wonder and reason in their mind, seeking what is right.
But it is so simple, the gift that was given.
Just take it and receive it from God in heaven.
Open the present set before you.
On Jesus's name, call.
Receive the gift of eternal life.
It is the greatest gift of all.

He Is Born

A story is forever told.
Its meaning forever unfolds.
The hope of all humankind fills the air
As the birth of Christ is celebrated everywhere.

All over the earth from north to south,
From sea to land and mountain high,
The sounds echo so faint and sweet,
"Glory to God in the Highest," as Christ's birth does yearly repeat.

For on this day many years ago,
A precious baby was born among the heavenly hosts.
His life's purpose few knew back then.
But questions and wonders about Him
Have never come to an end.

He is born.
And the story continues to be told
As the promise of salvation forever unfolds.

The Father's Heart

The Father's heart speaks too.
A gift from the Holy Spirit
I share with you.

Behind

Behind every hurt and pain,
Behind all your guilt and shame,
Behind all the fear and doubt,
God is there to lift you out.

Behind all of your crying and tears,
Behind all the broken years,
Behind it all, now look and see.
He is waiting to set you free.

God stands behind you, waiting patiently.
Do not let your life go fleetingly
To the wrong side of eternity.

Surrender all to Him,
And you will no longer be bound.
For in his arms,
Peace and love are found.

God is always waiting patiently.

Recovery Time

It is the dawning of a new day
As God's people lift their voices and pray
For America, land of the free,
Where God's grace was shed for all to see.

The hope of what can be
Is rising up in people's hearts
To see the vision clear.
Recovery time is here.

The body of Christ is awakening
From a long sleep.
Although during that time,
In God's grace He did keep.

No more slumbering, lack, or doubt.
It is time for God's people to come out.
Out against the attacks of persecution, ridicule, and shame
And from those who would slander His mighty name.

The mission is clear:
We are here to tell all that will hear,
"God so loved the world that He gave
His one and only Son, to save."

Stay focused and alert,
And with your eyes you will see
God's hand moving across this land,
To raise it up and make it His again!

God's Spirit

Hearken to God's voice.
Hearken to His ways.
As you do so,
He will guide your days.

Do not compromise or falter.
Lay all your burdens at the altar.
Then He can lead you well,
A life lived that will prevail.

You have within you
God's spirit sent from above.
No other creatures that have been created
Are saturated with this love.
Let His spirit lead and guide you
In all the things you do,
For then, no questions unanswered.
God's wisdom awaits you.

Believe

Limit God no more.
He always opens a door.
Believe Him for greater things.
Believe Him in everything.

For you are abiding in His vine.
God will pour out fresh new wine.
Stale nor tasteless, you will see
It will be like the sweetest honey.

Do not limit what He can do;
God will always see you through.
No more negative thoughts to cloud your mind;
Think positive in this day and time.

God is strong and mighty,
Not fragile or weak.
He created everything
By the words He did speak.

Act on His Word and believe it to be true,
And you will see mighty things come unto you.

You are never alone;
God is always near.
Call upon him;
He has a listening ear.

Never doubt God.
He will always be faithful to you.
Just believe that His Word is true.

Truth

God's one and only Son.
It is He
Who walked the streets in times past.
But men then did not see
The gift that was with them,
The truth that walked the land.
For He was the man wearing sandals,
The one with nailed, scarred hands.
He did it all, all He could do,
To save His children, yes, You.
He laid down His life; freely He did give
So that all could have eternal life and forever live.
Many turned away from Him
And received Him not.
They thought they knew the answers to life's lots,
Only to find out one day
That they knew nothing at all.
For when the end comes,
All humanity's ways will fall.
The only truth that will stand
Is the truth that Jesus saves and sets us free.
Just a simple man
Who walked the streets of Galilee.

No Other

Great and mighty are my God's ways.
He is the one who plans my days.
There is no other as great as He.
He is my heavenly Father.
He is my everything, you see.

No other can compare to Him.
He is the most loving of all.
Without Him, I would not be.
My God takes care of me.
He picks Me up, even when I fall.
He is my all in all.

In faraway lands, many call out to another.

There is no other.

He is the only way.
He alone is the only true God.
He is the God of the night and the day.

There is no other.

No other force can stand up against Him.
He is the creator and ruler of all.
For time alone is in His hand.
He has a plan and purpose for every man.

Seek God, no other,
While He can be found.
And believe in His Son, Jesus.
God will never let you down.

There is no other.

Harvest Time

Wake up, mighty men.
Turn from your wickedness and sin.
Sin no more and turn back in this hour.
Lead others to Christ and to His saving power.

Do not slumber any longer and do not sleep.
Harvest time has come, and it's time to reap.
Pull out the sickle and go forth with it in your hand.
Bring in every boy, girl, woman, and man.

For God will not move in the earth through another hand.
Only yours, the hand of man.
He does not wait to bring men in.
He waits on you to bring them in.

Move, mighty men and women of valor.
Get up and stop wasting time, doing what is shallow.
Step out deep into the river and see
All God has waiting for you and me.

Souls crying out for a saving hand.
Someone to lead them to the Father's hand.
There alone He will be,
Waiting for His precious fruit for all to see.

No more time to play.
Life and time are passing away.
Once He has brought His bride home,
The end will come quickly,
Many left behind.

But there is still hope for those
Whose blinders fall away,
For Christ's return will come soon.
Many awaiting that day.

Pray for the lost, that all may see
Before God shuts the Lamb's Book of Life
For all eternity.

Christ Return

The day is at hand.
The night is far spent.
For Jesus to come for his bride
For all who in Him abide.

All eyes will look toward the eastern sky
And see their redemption drawing nigh.
The light with its brightness
Will blind all who cannot see,
But those who are His,
With Christ Jesus they will be.

Many will think they see
A star from the sky exploding,
But those who know Him
Will see something different—love unfolding.

Crisis and havoc will overtake the earth
As his children arise from their place below
And meet Christ in the air,
Because it is Jesus that they know.

So be not afraid of what is coming your way.
Rejoice in Christ, your Lord, and say,
"My Savior is coming back for me,
And soon, and very soon that day will be!"

Scripture Reference

Today (PSALM 119:133)
A Clean Heart (PSALM 139:23 & 24)
My Day (PSALM 61:1)
I Am Free (ISAIAH 26:3)
Ways (EPHESIANS 6:10-18)
My Faith (PSALM 92:12)
Your Instrument (PSALM 92:1-4)
A Moment Of Time (PSALM 40:1)
He Is Listening (PHILIPPIANS 4:6)
Abide (PSALM 42)
Shadows (PSALM 91:3 & 4)
Behind The Scenes (II TIMOTHY 1:7)
Trust (PSALM 9:10)
Cares (MATTHEW 11:28-30)
Surely (JOHN 14:27)
Mercy (PSALM 91:14-16)
Cornerstones (EPHESIANS 6:19 & 20)
Harvest (MATTHEW 9:37 & 38)
Jesus Is Lord (JOHN 3:16)
Praying (EPHESIANS 6:18)
Love (I PETER 4:8)
Mighty Rush (ACTS 2:38 & 39)
The Way (I PETER 3:15)
Open Your Heart (I PETER 3:18)
Paid (HEBREWS 12:2-4)
Trip Of A Lifetime(I THESSALONIANS 4:16)
Zacchaeus (LUKE 19:1-10)
Heaven (PHILIPPIANS 3:20 & 21)
Are You Ready? (MATTHEW 25:8-13)
Love Is God (ROMANS 5:8)
God's Creation (PSALM 104:1-9 & 19-24)
Getting Up (GENESIS 1: 3-5)
At The Beach (GENESIS 1:10)
Lend A Hand (HEBREWS 13:16)

Reference

About the Author

Beth J. Rogers grew up in Georgia as a true southern girl. In high school, she served as the Vice President of the Georgia Future Homemakers of America. She and her husband, Mike, have two adult children and one grandchild and reside in Douglas, Georgia. Beth enjoys sports, music, writing, entertaining and spending time with family and friends.

Printed in the United States
By Bookmasters